CONTENTS

Introduction 3

Fear of Public Speaking 5

Breathe Your Fear Away and
Have a Commanding Voice As Well 9

How to Rehearse.. 15

Before Taking Your Show on the Road................................... 23

How to Power Your Presentations.. 25

How to Give Super Power Presentations
When You're Ready to Move to the Next Level.......................... 29

Taking Your Show on The Road.. 31

Encapsulation of Exercises 35

List of Verbs
(To Spur You to Action)... 39

INTRODUCTION

This handbook is about you.

It's about how to get the passionate you into your public speaking, instead of some idea of how a "business person" should give a presentation. The more you can ignite your passion for your presentation, the more products or services you will sell, or funds you will raise. Essentially your audience buys you, then your product.

What do I mean by the above? Let me give you an example. Perhaps you're a laid-back person, and you feel your really not cut out to be a good presenter or speaker. Now, laid-back is not a word we would use to describe Robert De Niro. He has a strong personality that has held our attention in scores of movies. This is the kind of strong persona that we usually feel we have to project to be a really good speaker—like Obama.

However, Kevin Costner, who definitely has a laid-back personality, has played in many kinds of films, including action movies. *He* certainly commands a lot of people's attention. How does he do that? How does a laid-back person become a star? He does it by releasing his passion without losing his natural personality. That's what I mean when I say this handbook is about getting the passionate you into your presentation, and not your idea of a "business person." (If you're trying to think of a laid back, yet very effective speaker, how about Bill Clinton?)

This handbook is not magic, but a nuts and bolts, step by step process, that frees the commanding speaker in you—no matter what you feel your talent to be. Toscanini, the virtuoso conductor, is claimed to have said, "Ninety percent talent, ten percent work, no good. Ten percent talent, ninety percent work, very good."

- If you want to speak with more power and conviction, no matter what your level of proficiency.

- If you're ready to experience that most good presenters are made, not born—both De Niro and Kostner studied acting, and yes, Obama and Clinton have been coached.

- If you've ever wanted to excite an audience with your presence and what you had to say—I wrote this handbook for you.

FEAR OF PUBLIC SPEAKING

Mitchell has just been announced as the presenter.

He gets up and starts walking to the front of the room. Mitchell's mind is jumbled, he's rapidly thinking, "Please don't make a mistake like last time, or forget something, or have a shaky voice in front of all these important people." His throat is dry and tense. He gets to the front of the room and turns to face the audience. All of a sudden his mind goes blank!

The above are some of the symptoms many people experience when they have to make a presentation. Fear of public speaking is a major obstacle to promotion and success in almost all professions. Studies have shown that it ranks right up there with fear of death! To quote Jerry Seinfeld, "According to most studies, people's number one fear is public speaking. Number two is death. Death is number two. Does that sound right? This means to the average person, if you go to a funeral, you're better off in the casket than doing the eulogy."

Fear of public speaking certainly tops the list of concerns that a good number of my clients have. So let's begin a journey that will take you from your fear, to looking forward to speaking, from your pounding heartbeat at the beginning of your presentation, to resounding applause at the end.

Practically everyone has a fear, or at least an anxiousness, when it comes to public speaking. It's only a matter of degree that separates them. But no matter how reluctant you may be, you can become a successful public speaker. I know this last statement may sound as realistic as your taking part in a Moon landing; but over the years I have worked with many fearful people, who have gone on to become successful public speakers in a relatively short period of time. You can become one of them.

HOW DID WE ACCOMPLISH THIS?

The short answer is by developing confidence. The longer answer is far more truthful. We accomplished this because my clients were willing to work through their fear to gain true confidence. That's the only way anyone truly gains confidence in anything—by doing what they're afraid of. To put it another way, my clients decided to do the eulogy.

Let's take a common example. Remember how you learned to ride a bike? You were probably nervous about performing the seemingly impossible task of balancing yourself on two wheels, while peddling and moving forward at the same time! Yet it was something that looked like fun, and all the other kids were doing it. You could travel far beyond your neighborhood if you wanted to. It represented a newfound freedom and you wanted to prove you were up to it. You may have had a lot of guidance and support, or little, or none at all. But in the end, you had to get on the bike and perform those seemingly impossible tasks, and risk falling in order to learn. After a number of tries it became easy. In other words, you took action and did what seemed impossible in order to ride a bicycle.

THE TRUTH IS ALWAYS SIMPLE.

My bicycle example may seem an obvious truth, yet not at all applicable to your fear of public speaking. However, let me synthesize a conversation I've had many times:

> **Client:** I get nervous speaking in public. My thoughts get jumbled. I trip over my words even when they're staring at me right there on the lectern! You know I'm pretty good one on one, but when there are more people, especially when I don't know them, I really get frazzled!

After listening to the client's specific problems, all of which are valid concerns, I ask this question:

> **Me:** How often do you rehearse?

> **Client:** Oh, I don't usually rehearse. I run over it in my head a few times.

> **Me:** Why don't you run over it out loud as if you were giving the presentation in front of an audience.

> **Client:** I never do that.

> **Me:** How come?

> **Client:** Well, now that you mention it, I can feel myself getting nervous just thinking about rehearsing the presentation as if I were in front of the audience.

> **Me:** Isn't that interesting. It seems to me that you have a vicious circle going on there. You don't rehearse out loud in front of an imaginary audience because that would make you nervous. But you know that when you get in front of an real audience you *will* get nervous. You see, you don't get any practice in dealing with your nervousness. That makes it really hard to get better—it's like trying to learn how to ride a bike without ever getting on the bike, let alone peddling.

IN A NUTSHELL, HOW YOU CAN LOSE YOUR FEAR

As simple as it may sound, it's true. I have helped people conquer their fear of public speaking by taking them through exercises that show them how to rehearse: how to prepare their material, how to find the message of the presentation, and how to use their passion to convey that message in the clearest, most compelling way. We all fear the unknown, so the more you know how to prepare your presentation, and what you want to convey with it, the less fear you will have. Let me tell you a story.

The fireman's fear

I once worked with a retired New York City fireman. He had been working at a large Wall Street firm for two years and was recently promoted to Director of Building Evacuation Procedure—after 9/11 this was not a go-through-the-motions position. Before he was to give evacuation procedure presentations to four different sections of the company, his supervisor thought it best that he give the presentation to a handful of people. He was so nervous during his talk that his supervisor had to come up and finish it for him. When he called me he was, understandably, frazzled—he had never given a presentation in his life! We had eight sessions in the space of two weeks because of his deadline. As you might imagine, the fireman had excellent motivation and discipline. I asked him to please call me when he finished the presentations—he had to give all four on the same day. When he called he was so excited about his success, I had to hold the phone at almost arms length. He said he surprised everyone, his supervisor called it miraculous.

The how of rehearsing

As the fireman experienced, rehearsing is not just saying your speech over and over again so you won't make any mistakes. This kind of rote memorization, or extemporizing on your bullet points can easily lead to a mind-numbing, predictable presentation. Knowing how to rehearse makes you more involved with the message you are conveying to your audience, and less involved with your fear of *not* conveying it, or making a mistake. It takes your focus away from your inward-looking fear, and turns that focus outward toward your message and the audience. If you don't feed the fire of your fear with your attention, it won't burn.

Some people say they don't want to get too familiar with their presentation, because then they'll sound as if they memorized it. Even if you went as far as memorizing it, it would not *sound* memorized if you are more focused on what you are trying to convey, than getting it word for word perfect. Again, you take your inward focus about getting it perfect, and turn your focus outward to the audience. No one in your audience knows or cares if it's word perfect. They care if it's engaging.

You may immediately want to know how to rehearse, even if you doubt it will work. However, what I first show a client is not how to rehearse, but something that will make them less fearful and more confident in the very first session. I teach them how to breathe.

BREATHE YOUR FEAR AWAY
And Have A Commanding Voice As Well

"Wait a second. Slow down and take a breath!"

Sound familiar? Something like those words have been said by, or to, most of us. This common expression speaks volumes about our innate wisdom—we intuitively know that breath relaxes. What may not be as obvious is that breath can also give support and command to your voice.

Virtually all public speaking courses neglect to teach correct breathing, or give it barely a mention. Yet breath is the foundation of speech. When we speak, the air in our lungs rises and vibrates our vocal cords. If your breathing isn't deep and supported, your voice, which is dependent on the strength of your breath, will be weakened and go up in pitch. This happens to many people because they habitually take shallow breaths.

When stressed, which many of us are on a daily basis, we tense our jaws, shoulders, stomach, etc. This makes us take shallow breaths. Some degree of stress is common when speaking in public, so if your breathing is shallow to begin with, it becomes even more constricted. When this happens, you can't think clearly for lack of sufficient oxygen, you might feel tightness in your chest, and your words can come out in a rush.

Conversely, breathing well is a universally known relaxant. Beside the above-mentioned common expression, breath is a relaxation cornerstone in Yoga, the martial arts, Pilates, Transcendental Meditation, and numerous other disciplines. And breath is essential in giving you the support for a commanding vocal presence—as any professional singer knows. So it's important for a speaker to learn at least the basics of correct breathing. Let's take a look at how natural diaphragmatic breathing works.

LOOK AT YOURSELF

Stand in front of a mirror in which you can see yourself from the waist up—now would be a great time to do this. Take a deep breath and notice where the air goes as it enters your body. The vast majority of people who try this will see their chest rise when they inhale. Unfortunately, most of us breathe this shallow way.

Think back to when you were last frightened—you gasped an intake of air, your chest rose, and you held your breath. When we breathe into our chests in this shallow way, it mimics that frightened state, and makes us less relaxed. We tend to breathe this way when under stress, which creates more stress. Again, stress is common when speaking, so if you tend to breathe shallowly to begin with, it makes it impossible to deliver the compelling speech you're capable of. When in this state, you feel like you're running out of air and can't finish a sentence. For some, it leaves them inwardly flailing for air, as if they were drowning in a sea of words.

BREATH AND RELAXATION

Now for something I think you'll find more pleasurable. If you do the following, you will not only be more relaxed, but you will impress yourself with the sounds you create. *(All of the following exercises will be encapsulated in the back of this handbook for easy reference.)*

Reaching for the ceiling

In preparation to doing the following breathing exercises, do this one exercise to help stretch the muscles that allow your ribcage to move.

1. Standing, with your arms at your sides, look up at the ceiling and slowly reach for it as if you're trying to touch it, first with your left hand, then as your bringing your left hand down, start reaching with your right. Really reach, but gently. There's a tendency to stop breathing during this exercise, especially when you're at the top of your reach. Keep breathing! Do this three times on each side. Then relax, with arms at your sides.

2. Repeat all of the above two more times.

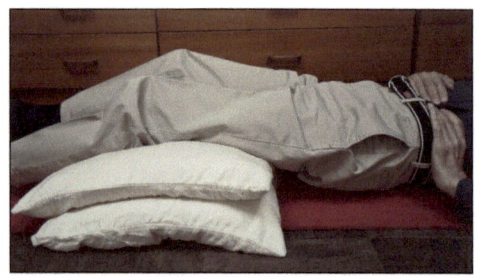

Breathe your stress away

Lie down on your back on a comfortable mat, towel or carpet. Place a small pillow under your head; then as pictured above, a large pillow, or several pillows under your calves. The pillow(s) under your calves will take some of the curve out of your lower back and help you relax. (Instead of the pillows under your calves, you can also point your knees at the ceiling with your feet flat on the floor, but most find the other position to be relaxation heaven.)

1. Let your arms relax comfortably by your sides. Close your eyes and give yourself several minutes to just relax, breathing in and out through your nose. Let all your tensions dissolve from your head to the base of your spine. Let your face, your neck, your spine, chest and stomach relax. Take your time. You're melting into the mat like a pat of butter in a warm pan. Feel your spine relax all the way from the nape of your neck to the base of your spine. Keep relaxing for three to five minutes, or more if you like, feeling as if your whole upper body is sighing into the floor. It's very helpful to use a timer, but keep it very close at hand so you barely have to move to stop it—the softer the alarm sound, the better.

2. Now, gently feel where your breath is going. Chances are your breath is much lower in your body than your upper chest; in fact your stomach is probably rising and falling. When we relax, we naturally

breathe this way. It's easier to get in touch with our natural breathing when we're lying down and letting go of tension—we breathe this way when we sleep.

Diaphragmatic breathing

What happens when you relax is that you free your diaphragm to perform its natural function. The diaphragm is a sheet of muscle that separates your chest from your abdomen. When the diaphragm contracts and descends, breath is drawn down into the lowest part of the lungs. You cannot feel your diaphragm directly, but as it descends you can feel it displacing your stomach, causing your stomach to rise with each inhalation and fall with each exhalation. If you are tense, your diaphragm can't descend and your breath will be shallow and confined to your chest.

1. As diaphragmatic breathing becomes more familiar to you, feel if the muscles between your lower ribs are allowing your lower rib cage to expand with your inhalation, and contract with your exhalation. As pictured above, you check this by placing one hand on your lower ribs (thumb around back touching your lower ribs where they bulge the most, your other fingers around your front ribs). If your lower ribs are not moving yet, don't worry, just keep doing the "reaching for the ceiling" exercise and they will. You can also place a hand on your stomach to feel its movement. All of this together: your diaphragm descending and rising, your stomach rising and falling and your lower rib cage expanding and contracting, is called diaphragmatic breathing.

2. As you breathe, notice if your upper chest is moving less than when you took a breath looking in the mirror. It should hardly move at all, but don't expect that to happen right away. (There will always be some natural movement because your

chest, of course, is part of your ribcage, the lower part of which is in motion.) If you concentrate on feeling your breath go down into the bottom of your torso, your upper chest will move less and less. Literally think your breath, and feel your breath going down to below your naval; you will only create more tension by trying to force it there. Gently breathe like this for three to five minutes. Get as strong a bodily feeling as you can in terms of what diaphragmatic breathing feels like. The more you practice, the more automatic this will become, to the point where you can literally forget about it and let your body take over—remember, your body wants to breathe this natural way. When your breath comes from the deep descent of the diaphragm, your voice will have a presence and command that will compel an audience to listen.

Diaphragmatic breathing is the correct way to breathe for sustained, resonant, commanding speech. Your speech is sustained because it is rooted in the diaphragm, and it is resonant and commanding because of the vibrations it causes in your rib cage, back, and chest. In short, your voice is coming from your whole torso, as opposed to your head and upper chest. Later on in this exercise when you start to add sound to your exhalation, you will actually feel the vibrations with the hand you've placed on your lower chest. You should also feel some vibration in your rib cage—if you do not at first, you will in time. Your body will become an echo chamber similar to the one you enjoy while singing in the shower. If you don't sing in the shower, you have experienced your voice this way the last time you burst out laughing. Your laugh was rich and full. This kind of laugh is commonly called a belly laugh. When you have a good belly laugh you have been spontaneously surprised into breathing correctly.

Remember how relaxed you felt when you finished laughing?

It's a good idea to watch your breathing every time you're on the phone; I think you may be surprised to find yourself holding your breath, particularly when it's a stressful call. If you know the call will be stressful, that's a red flag saying, "really watch your breathing." This will improve your breathing by getting your awareness of it into your everyday life. Also, it will make you calmer, and give you a greater phone presence.

OPENING THE "DOORS" TO LET THE MOST SOUND OUT

OK, so you've practiced diaphragmatic breathing for three to five minutes. Let's now do a couple of very helpful movement exercises from right where you are on the floor. I suggest these exercises be done just before any speaking engagement. They are, as you will see, soundless, and can be done practically anywhere, whether you're lying down, seated or standing. Many executives do these two exercises just before they speak. They don't do them just because I tell them to, but because they've experienced that they work.

Door 1: How to relax your mouth to let more sound out

The first door to open is your jaw. Most people's jaws are tight, and that leads to limiting the power of the sound that comes out of them—think of all those open mouth, belting singers that you've seen. Become aware of how your jaw feels. Now, what I'd like you to do is imagine that you're eating something that is delicious and chewy. With your lips touching, chew "it" for a full minute, remember it's delicious so really chew and savor what you're eating. Time yourself, because a minute is much longer than most of us think. When you've finished, your jaw will probably be tired but also more relaxed, and therefore more capable of greater movement, which

is the goal of this exercise. Compare how it feels now, to before you did the exercise. The more open and free your jaw is, the more you allow your full sound to emerge. No, I'm not suggesting that your jaw should be as open as a singer's, just a little more than usual.

Door 2: How to relax your palate so we hear all about it

The second exercise involves the other "door" you have, your soft palate. That's the opening just behind your tongue that has that fleshy extension hanging from it called the Uvula—the thing that you see vibrating wildly in all the cartoons that have a cat or someone screaming as the camera peers down their throat. Stretch your soft palate by yawning. Stretch your arms above your head and yawn. If you find yourself yawning for real, that's great, you're relaxing more. Yawn several times feeling your soft palate stretch.

Again, our soft palates are too tense, and stretching them makes them relax. Have you ever talked while you're yawning? I'll bet your voice was fuller and deeper sounding. Opening your soft palate helps create that full, resonant sound. Stretching and yawning is great to do several times during the day; apart from helping your ribs to vibrate making that more resonant sound, it relaxes you. It also stretches your rib muscles, which gives more movement to your ribcage, resulting in fuller, deeper breaths. So the fuller voice is the result of stretching, breathing deeper and relaxing. Again, I strongly suggest you do these two exercises as close to your speaking time as possible. I know perfectly normal people in all levels of business, who do them in rest room cubicles just before speaking.

MAKING SOUNDS RESOUND

Do each of the following exercises for a minute or two, looking for the sound to emanate from deep in your torso.

1. Again, place one hand on your lower ribs (thumb around back touching your lower ribs where they bulge the most, your other fingers around your front ribs), and place your other hand on your stomach. Diaphragmatically breathe all the way down, except breathe in and out through your mouth because that's the way we breathe when we speak or make sounds. Once you've breathed in, make the sound, HAH-HAH-HAH. This should be a short sound that you gently create with your breath from deep down in your torso—feel as if the sound were coming from below your navel. The AH is the same open sound as in discovering something, AH! You're just adding an H to it. Repeat the HAH-HAH-HAH several times with a breath between each set of three HAH's. Notice that your stomach is bouncing with each sound. That bounce is your diaphragm and stomach muscles automatically supporting the sound. You didn't "do" anything to make that bounce, except that when you breathe down into your lower torso and touch the sound off from there, you naturally get that support.

2. Next try to hold that HAH sound a little longer by chanting it—drawing it out. Again you should be creating the sound from below your navel, like softly beating a drum, HAAAAH (breath) HAAAAH (breath) HAAAAH. Hold the A vowel for a few seconds. Feel the sound reverberating in your body as if your shower stall were in you, or as if your body were a huge resounding cathedral. You might want to shift your rib cage hand up to your chest to feel the vibrations there. Then you could move the same hand back to your lower rib cage to see how much you are vibrating there. Again, don't be discouraged if you feel little, or no movement or vibration in your lower ribs at first. Just gently keep thinking the sound down, and doing the "reaching for the ceiling" exercise, and it will come.

3. Lastly, make the sound MUM (like the first syllable in mum-ble). Do this in sets of three: MUM-MUM-MUM making short sounds at first, then longer chanting sounds. Hold the U vowel for a few seconds: MUUUUM. Make sure you're breathing when you need to. You don't want to be totally running out of breath before you breathe again. The M sound gives you lots of humming and resonance, and will help you get more in touch with the full rich sound you're gently looking for. Check your ribcage, because there's a greater chance that you might be vibrating there if you weren't before. Remember this takes a little practice.

The below is a three-step process: lying down, seated, and standing. What you're looking for while seated or standing, is to have your voice sound similar to the way it sounds when you're lying down. Of course to achieve this you need the same level of relaxation and breathing that you had lying down. It's a matter of becoming aware of how you physically feel when you're lying down and relaxing/breathing well, and then gradually translating that feeling into the other postures. Your voice may sound strange to you at first, but as you relax into it, you will begin to realize it is the strong supported voice you've had in you all along. It's just been waiting to come out.

SAYING YOUR FIRST WORDS

Now, while still lying down, you're ready to say some words:

1. You could imagine introducing yourself to a group of business people, giving your name and position and what you do in your company—"Good Morning, I'm Peter Simon, Sales Spokesperson for Diamond Investments. I'd first like to

thank you for the opportunity to speak about why you should invest with Diamond." Or you could recite some lines from a favorite poem, song, or speech. Keep your hands where they were in the previous exercise. Remember to breathe, feeling the movement in your stomach and ribcage. Notice if your voice sounds different. It most likely will be at least somewhat fuller or richer, more like the voice you might have when you first get up in the morning. This so called "morning voice" occurs when you wake up relaxed after a good nights sleep, and you're breathing much better than you are later on in your stressful day.

Then chant (draw out) each word holding it a little longer, as you did with the sounds above, while speaking the same passage. Notice the extra energy that chanting requires.

Then do the passage in your normal voice, but using the same energy that you used to chant. You might be surprised that doing the chanting improved your more normal voice. I say more normal voice because public speaking requires your normal voice but at a higher energy level. While this energy will make your voice sound louder, because of your newfound resonance, it is a far cry from shouting.

2. Carefully get up and sit in a straight-backed chair. (I say carefully because you might be a little light headed from all the oxygen you've taken in.) Try to sit as erect as possible without causing unnecessary tension, and repeat whatever words you just said while lying down. Don't forget to breathe. See how much of your fuller sound you have retained from your previous position. Then, as before, chant this passage and then go back to your more normal voice, again keeping the energy of the chanting.

3. Now stand as straight as you can without unnecessary tension and repeat the words you spoke, again noticing any differences. Don't forget to then chant the same words and feel the energy it demands. Then again your more normal voice, but keeping the energy it took to chant. If you feel like you're shouting, you're trying too hard. Public speaking takes a lot of energy but not a bit of force or tension.

TAKING STEPS

Speaking, like everything else that's worth doing, is all about practice and patience. But I assure you, if you want to be an effective, compelling speaker, this handbook points out the quickest way there. The exercises and suggestions in this handbook will help you be a better speaker step by small step—it's the way we learned to walk and it can't be improved upon. If you follow these steps and put them into practice with a live audience, you will see a marked improvement in your speaking. Will your fear or anxiousness totally go away? No. That would be unrealistic. Also, if your fear totally went away, that would prevent you from becoming the vital, commanding speaker you want to be. You need some fear (anxiousness, nervousness, adrenaline rush or whatever you want to call it) to focus and use so you're the most alive person in the room—that's when audiences really listen. So, through these exercises, and practicing your presentation, and speaking in public, your fear will lessen to the point that it becomes a powerful ally.

HOW TO REHEARSE

The structure of a presentation.

In preparing for a presentation,

the first thing to understand is it's

basic structure. We know that every

story has a beginning, middle, and

an end. Presentations are similar:

there's the introduction, body, and

closing.

The popular phrase describing what you do for presentations or speeches is: "Say what you're going to say, say it, then say what you just said." If this works for you, by all means use it. It's a good rule of thumb.

However, I prefer the following because it can stir the imagination.

Introduction

The introduction is usually an overview of what you are going to talk about. It's where you "set-up" the audience for the great story you have in store for them. It's like the coming attraction, or trailer that lets you in on the highlights of a movie.

Body

The body is the telling of the full story that you highlighted in the introduction.

Closing

The closing is a wrapping up of all the important elements of your story, making sure that the audience gets the story's full weight: the message you are conveying in order to spur them to action.

TELL ME A STORY

I've just referred to a presentation as a story. No matter what you've been handed or personally written to present, every conceivable type of presentation *is* a story. I can't begin to tell you how many times a client has come to me and said, "I have this boring financial report to give." I reply that they should never give a report in a presentation. Reports are boring. Stories are not. There is not a culture in the world that doesn't have story telling as a treasured part of their lives. Everyone loves a good story well told.

And there's a story in every financial report. Let me give you an example: There's where you started, then because you positioned yourselves well, your stock soared. Then this financial crunch happened and your stock plummeted. Then, in order to dig yourselves out of the hole you were in you did this. But that was failing… Until!! No matter how stiffly a presentation is written, you can pull the story out of it and make it at least interesting if not a cliffhanger.

So it's important right from the get-go that you get into a storytelling frame of mind. If you find it difficult getting into this frame of mind, just think back to when you told a story to friends at a party, or while you were having a drink with associates around a table. You were feeling relaxed and you felt the story was really interesting or funny and wanted to share it. The feeling that compels you to tell the story is: *I've got to tell you this!* It also compels them to listen.

If you're more on the shy side, think of when you had to tell a delicious story to a close friend. In either case bring that *I've got to tell you this* storytelling feeling to your presentation. It will make for a far more engrossing experience for you and your audience.

HOW STORYTELLING AFFECTS YOUR PRESENTATION

Thinking of your presentation as a story begs you to pay close attention to its twists and turns—the shifts from one topic to another and their level of importance to the story as a whole. The storytelling frame of mind will also be a great help if you're writing your presentation, or have some input into the writing. So first look over your presentation in order to explore what would make the audience want to listen—this is one of the things the storytelling frame of mind does—it compels you to think not only about what you want to convey, but how and to whom you're going

to convey it.

For instance: I once worked with the head of an IT department who had to give the identical presentation, on separate occasions, to the IT department and then to upper management. Using the storytelling perspective, he accented the technical side of the presentation, and softened the bottom line aspect, when speaking to the IT department—also his approach was casual. His more formal telling of the same story was just the reverse for upper management. He accented the bottom line and softened the technical side.

If the only thing you got from this handbook were the ability to conceptualize your presentation as a story, and convey it as such, you would markedly improve your public speaking.

THE POWER OF "AS IF"

I will be referring to *as if* quite a bit from now on. The power of *as if* is that you don't try to convince yourself you're doing whatever you're imagining. You're just going to do it *as if* what you're imagining were so. For example: when you're rehearsing you speak as if there were an audience. By not trying to convince yourself, it becomes easier to act like an audience is there.

TALKING TO YOURSELF

The next thing to do after giving your presentation some storytelling thought is to say it out loud, with the kind of energy you would have in front of an audience—at this point you don't have to refer to the audience. Just say it out loud *as if* the audience were there. Reading is one thing. Saying your story out loud is quite another. The story sounds different as you speak it. It demands you give it immediacy and clarity, because the audience has to get it the first time. If you do this, you will undoubtedly find better ways of getting your message across. If you're writing your presentation you might even change whole sections, or move sections around, because of saying it out loud and as a story. This stage overlaps with the next: beginning to rehearse.

REHEARSING

The rehearsal period is a good time to refine the message of your story. What is your goal or objective in telling this story? Naturally, if you were a thingamajig seller you would love to *sell* a thingamajig to everyone in the audience, and all of their relatives and friends. However, this is not a good objective because it's all about *your* needs and doesn't include the audience's needs. Just think of a time when someone *tried* to sell you something. It most likely pushed you away. That's what you would do to the audience if your objective were to try to sell them something without considering them.

I'm not talking about changing the words of a presentation that was created for you to deliver as is, except for your clarifying comments. I'm talking about changing the *action* behind saying the words. Lets say you ask someone to do something and their reply is, "I'll do it." But they leave you with the feeling that they *won't* do it. Their action would be *to dismiss* or *to slough off* your request. Their action to disregard your request is in their voice and body language and the feeling they convey. Another person could respond with the same words, "I'll do it," but leave you with the feeling that it's as good as done. Their action would be *to assure* you or *to affirm* their commitment.

It's amazing what different effects you can have on an audience using the same words but with a different action.

FINDING THE OBJECTIVE

Again, your objective should present your product or service in a way that would include the audience's needs, and therefore their interest. The best thing to do to find your objective is to think of the story of your product. Instead of trying to sell the audience something, your objective might be: to stimulate their need for your product or service. This objective would make it imperative that you tell the story of your product with clear-eyed attention to its advantages, and how these advantages would fulfill a need in your audience. So this objective would make the story more compelling for you and your audience, and also fulfill your needs—to sell a lot of thingamajigs.

The above is a good example to keep in mind: the wording and pursuit of objectives is very individual. I chose to *stimulate* need for the product. For a different salesperson, *to generate* sales might be just the ticket, as long as his or her understanding of *to generate* sales got their passion flowing, and included the needs of the audience.

So the objective you choose to pursue is very important. To quote Peter Drucker, the widely read writer and management consultant, "Management by objectives works if you first think through your objectives. Ninety percent of the time you haven't." The same holds true for every kind of public speaking. Suppose a person giving an academic talk on the history of the freedoms we enjoy in America, chose as his or her objective, *to give* information, as opposed to, *to inspire* the audience. If you were in the audience, which objective would you want the speaker to pursue? Do you think if you were inspired, you would also receive the information?

When you find the right objective you'll feel that "special something" you feel when you know, "This is a yes!" You'll feel grounded in your speech. At the same time, you'll feel ready to fly. But to fly to your objective, you're going to have to know the flight plan you intend to use to reach it.

GOING TO CHICAGO

If you're objective were to fly to Chicago, you would have to take a number of actions in order to get there. You would have *to set* a date, *to make* a reservation, and *to pack* a bag, to mention a few. Similarly, once you have an objective for your presentation, you have to find out what actions you are going to take to get you and your audience to arrive at your "Chicago."

Let's take the objective I used before as an example: *to stimulate* the audience's need for your product or service. If the only action you took in pursuing this objective was *to point out* this advantage, then this advantage, then this advantage… I think you get the point, it would become, at the very least, repetitious. You have a good objective. Now you must ask yourself, "How do I get my audience to my objective?" Let's say you open your presentation with the action: *to arouse* their curiosity— this could be a nice light way to begin. You could do this by posing a rhetorical question, or telling an interesting story about the product, or how you got interested in selling the product or service. People would start to lean towards you because they want you to fill in the blanks posed by your question, or because they want to hear how your interesting story ends. You could follow that segment of your speech with, *to illustrate or demonstrate* your products' design and practicality, or ease of handling. With your next segment you could choose, *to impress* upon them its dependability and customer satisfaction, or its quality and back-up service. Each of these actions could be done in a few sentences worked into your existing Power Point bullet points—providing the actions are relevant to the slide you're on.

Also, all of these actions pursue the objective, *to stimulate* the audience's need for your product. Together they add a great deal of variety and interest to your presentation, thus avoiding a one-note appeal.

The above holds true no matter what you're speaking about—whether selling a product or service, or seeking donations for a charitable institution. Surely every life or business endeavor should have an objective in mind, and a plan of action on how to get there. For instance: You intend to become a better public speaker—that is your objective. Your actions would be to read this book and *to practice* what it says.

EVERY SPEECH IS LIKE AN ACTION MOVIE

As in a good action movie, a speech must do something to the audience. In the above section, all the actions I chose, and the objective they are meant to pursue, are verbs: '*to arouse* their curiosity,' '*to illustrate* or *demonstrate*,' and '*to impress*.' These are words that spur action. Any audience intuitively follows not just your words but also the action you pursue as you say them. We all do this in our everyday conversations. The 'I'll do it' example, I gave earlier illustrates this. But here's another: The boss, Peter, asks Jim, the head of Shipping and Receiving, "That order is supposed to come in on the 13th right?" He says it in such a way though, that his action is *to pin* Jim down to that delivery date—as opposed to simply asking what the shipper promised. Jim answers, "That's what he said. But he's been late before." I think most of us know Jim's action: *to cover* his posterior. Our actions tell the audience what we mean by what we say. So you must be affecting the audience with your words, not just making sense. And what you're doing (your action) must be consistent with what you want to convey. Speaking clearly and coherently is important, but without an action that springs the words forward toward your goal or objective, your speech falls flat, or is misunderstood. To quote an old saying: "It ain't what you say, it's how you say it." My contention is: It is what you say *and* it's how you say it. The how you say it is what this handbook is mainly about.

There's a list of verbs you could use for actions or objectives at the back of this handbook.

VISUALIZING YOU'RE IMAGINED AUDIENCE

By an imagined audience I mean just that. This is where your imagination, correct breathing, and relaxation techniques come together.

Several decades ago, scientists discovered that when we imagine something, it has a measurable effect on our nervous system and musculature. Now, top athletes routinely use this knowledge to improve their game. Tennis pros, to football players, use what is called: *Visualization*. Whether it is to improve their serve, or their running game, visualization is a widely accepted tool. It conditions and acclimates your nervous system to an actual act you will be doing. Seasoned presenters use visualization routinely. It is also used in many medical settings, to help people control anxiety attacks, and many other conditions.

WHAT EXACTLY IS VISUALIZATION

Remember your last pleasant dream and you'll remember how good you felt when you woke. Of course, a nightmare has woken most of us with our hearts pounding and the eerie feeling that it really happened. In both dreams we had not actually done anything, but our bodies reacted *as if* we had. Visualization is in many ways conscious dreaming. We visualize something *as if* it were really happening, so we can improve a real life circumstance.

Those who have already done the breathing exercises have experienced how breathing can help you relax. The visualization exercise I'm about to take you through will, in a relatively short amount of time, help you to relax in the moments just before you make a presentation.

Visualization Exercise

1. Sit down and close your eyes, and breathe in and out through your nose. Make sure you are gently breathing down into your lower torso. Feel your feet flat on the floor—no crossed legs as that just ties you up and creates tension. Feel your buttocks on the chair. Become aware of all of the following at once: gently inhaling all the way down, and exhaling, feet flat on the floor, and your seat on your chair. This is not so much a breathing exercise as you did before, but an awareness of your body, and breathing, and your physical presence in the chair.

2. Now imagine that the chair you're sitting in is in the room or auditorium, in which you're going to make your presentation. You're watching and listening to the person who is about to introduce you. It's important that you are not watching yourself as if you were in a movie. Rather, you are in the room looking out of your eyes at this person. You're aware of your breathing, feeling yourself in the chair, and listening to the speaker.

   • At this point you might feel yourself getting anxious, *as if* you were really about to speak. Your mind may wander, perhaps becoming concerned about your talk. That's OK. It's what a lot of speakers do—that is, not really listening to the speaker who's introducing them, but listening to their own fear or anxiousness. *That's why you're doing this visualization.* It's a rehearsal for the real thing. It will get you used to those moments just before you speak, and embed in your mind and nervous system, what you can do to counter your fear when you're in the actual situation. *What you can do when your mind begins to wander, is don't give yourself a hard time, just gently bring yourself back to your breathing, feeling yourself in your chair, and listening to the speaker.* By doing this you are staying in the present, and not two or three steps ahead worrying if it's going to go all right.

Change the following to suit the physical layout and the protocols of your speaking engagement. Maintain looking out of your eyes and not watching yourself. You do not physically get up, but do all of the following in your imagination.

1. When the speaker introduces you, imagine yourself pushing your chair back, getting up and walking to the lectern. Be aware of your walking, and breathing, and the applause. As you approach the person who has introduced you, look him or her in the eye, shake hands and thank the person. Step 2 is a moment of truth for a lot of speakers.

2. In your visualization, imagine yourself turning and facing your audience. The first thing you do is to look directly at a friendly face somewhere mid-audience, and take a breath (you can pick out a friendly face before you get up to speak). You do not hold your breath and hurriedly launch into your presentation. In the second or two that it takes you to breathe, you give the audience a chance to see you—I know, it will seem like an eternity. Believe me, it's not. The audience will feel you're calm and confident because you're taking your time. Now *imagine* yourself saying the opening remarks of your presentation—you "say them" in a welcoming way, as if you were inviting guests into a gathering at your home. When you finish imagining your opening remarks, gently bring yourself out of your visualization and open your eyes.

You'll probably feel more relaxed when you open your eyes. This is because you have constantly been bringing yourself back to the present when your mind started to wander to your worries and fears. You have been breathing, rather than bracing yourself and not breathing. And that has made you more relaxed and able to focus your nervous energy on your presentation.

The more you rehearse by doing this visualization, the more familiar your whole being (your mind, your nervous system, and musculature) will become with what to do in the few minutes before you get up to speak. As I've said, we are most afraid of what we don't know, and this is a very important way to make us more familiar with speaking.

Doing what you visualized—walk to the lectern

Next you should physically do what you visualized. In this example we're going to presume it's a speech given at a lectern. In the room where you are rehearsing set an actual place where the lectern is—you can buy an inexpensive portable music stand to serve as a lectern. Then you should:

1. Imagine that you are being announced (you are breathing, feeling yourself in the chair, and watching the spot where you put the lectern)

2. Then you actually get up and walk to the lectern, being aware of any possible obstacles, like cables, chair legs etc., then shake an imaginary hand while you look your "greeter" in the eye

3. Turn and face the "audience," seek out a "friendly face" while you take a breath

4. Start your presentation

Although the above may sound somewhat strange, if you do it as often as practical, you will be amazed how much it will reduce, and/or focus your fear in the actual situation. It's no different than baseball players visualizing certain plays and then actually practicing them over and over again until they are second nature: with a runner on first, a ground ball is hit to the shortstop, who soft tosses it to the second baseman, who, while avoiding the runner sliding into him, throws to first. When the real game comes, no matter what the pressure, they are prepared to react when the double play presents itself. If you don't know, this is exactly what many real-life baseball players do. Mock battles serve the same purpose for soldiers. Practice can never be the same as the real thing, but it can prepare you for the real thing so it isn't overwhelming. So practice the beginning of your speech often. It will get you off to a good start.

RELAXATION IS CONTAGIOUS

When you have a good start, your audience relaxes because they feel you are confident. Remembering to take a breath as you initially look at your audience gives them a chance to see you, and sense that you don't look nervous or rushed—although you may have a million butterflies fluttering around in your stomach. If you start rushed, your audience will feel anxious for you. I'm sure you've felt uneasy while you were watching a rushed and nervous speaker. Take a breath, and your time with the beginning of your speech, and see how contagious a relaxed beginning can be. Nervousness is contagious, but relaxation is even more so. Why? Because nobody comes to see a bad presentation anymore than you go to a movie hoping that it's bad. So the audience wants to be relaxed, and you to be engaging. Being engaging is closely related to being prepared.

"MAKING MISTAKES"

My heading is in quotation marks, because most mistakes speakers are aware of are not noticeable to an audience, or are not important to them—you missed a word in your talk that they don't know you missed, or you stumble over a sentence. If you make a big deal about it, then it *will* be a big deal. But if you take a breath, regain your focus, and stay with what you're now saying, instead of your mind being back at the "mistake," you'll keep moving forward in pursuit of your objective. And if it was a noticeable mistake, the audience will think the better of you if you appear unruffled by it. You could have a line ready for a really big gaffe. For instance, if something you said was totally incomprehensible you could say, "Wasn't *that* an interesting sentence? What I meant was... The point is not to make a big deal of it, and believe me, the audience won't either. Usually it's best not to say anything, or at most, excuse me, take a breath, focus and move on.

Too many of us wander into public speaking and don't prepare enough to reap it's full rewards. There's an ancient Chinese saying that goes, "If you walk into a lion's den, be prepared to meet a lion." Well, for a lot of us, public speaking is a lion's den, and if we are going to walk into it, we'd better be prepared for the richly rewarding adventure of taming that lion, and harnessing it's power.

BEFORE TAKING YOUR SHOW ON THE ROAD

OK, so you've practiced your breathing,

exercised your jaw and soft palette

two or three times each day,

you've visualized the two or three

minutes before you're going to be

introduced two or three times a day,

you've physically done what you've

visualized and said the first few

lines of your presentation as much

as possible.

You've also been familiarizing yourself with the rest of the presentation by reading it out loud and thinking about your objective. Then, you've experimented with actions that you feel will get you to that objective. What's next?

DO I HAVE TO MEMORIZE MY PRESENTATION?

This question comes up a lot as I'm working with clients. You have to discover what works best for you. Most people work off their bullet points, but I make sure that they are very familiar with what they are going to say. I discourage memorizing it word for word, because if you miss a few words you tend to be distracted by it. However, you should have your opening and closing unforgettably memorized—this gives you a confidence building solid beginning and ending.

If you're not working with Power Point and referring to your computer, you can make a small list of points on an index card or cards. You can place them on the conference table in front of you, or on the lectern, whatever the case may be.

PREPARING YOUR HARD COPY

You could even place a whole speech in front of you for reference. If you do this, I suggest the following:

1. Your text should be at least 14 point type so you can refer to it at a glance. You can double-space the text if the speech is not long, or else you'll be dealing with a lot of pages.

2. In the actual circumstance, do not spend most of your time reading a speech from a script, unless you want the audience to only remember the top of your head. So be very familiar with what is on the page.

3. For speaking purposes never staple pages together. Always have two pages in front of you, that way when you're finished with page one, you can refer to page two without distracting the audience by noisily turning pages. Also, while you speak from familiarity the words that are on page two, you can soundlessly move it over to the right on top of page one. Again you will have two pages in front of you.

4. In going from one page to another you can break the text in whatever way is most clear to you. I recommend that you mark your text, or highlight it, in places where you have trouble, or want to strongly emphasize.

PRACTICING—ALWAYS OUT LOUD *AS IF* YOU HAD AN AUDIENCE

Practice whatever way you're going to work. For instance, if you're doing a power point presentation use your personal computer and work off that. Or if you're working from a script, practice how to quickly pick up the words, or part you don't know, so you can contact the audience again—if you're having trouble, try making the font bigger. As you're doing all of this the speech is becoming more and more familiar.

Now is the time to dig deeper.

HOW TO POWER YOUR PRESENTATIONS

Two pieces of advice:

The first: listen to your heart and it will lead the way.

The second: Don't put your heart above your head.

Heart and head are often seen as opposites. For some people heads are more reliable, for others, hearts.

As far as I'm concerned, heads can be as unreliable as hearts. It's when you get the two together that you have something to lean on in life or in a speech. If a speech is all head, it's going to be dry and not very inviting. If it's all heart, it will probably lack clarity. So it's good to have both heart and head in your speech. Your head provides the information in a clear way, and your heart provides the personal connection to your audience. If you're in the audience, a "heart and head" speech is like a good movie: you know exactly what's going on as you reach for your Kleenex. Or laugh. Or wonder. Or be informed. Your heart and head together are like the positive and negative in electricity—they power the words you say.

IS THIS ANY WAY TO DO BUSINESS?

It's the *only* way to do business. Too often we approach a business talk like, well, business. You say, "I mean after all, this is business isn't it?" Yes, it is, and we're not going to forget that. What we should remember is that business is conducted by human beings, no exceptions. And you can reach them deeply with your message only through both their hearts and heads. Even if you're talking high finance, do you think it would work to your advantage if they thought you were bright *and* likable? And would be wonderful to work with?

HOW DO YOU GET BOTH HEART AND HEAD IN YOUR PRESENTATION?

We're back to the objective and actions again. Only now you have a deeper experiential knowledge of your presentation. Again look at the *why* of your speech. Have your head ask your heart, "Why am I saying this? What is my objective?" With your new familiarity of your presentation, really ask yourself this question, and rummage around in your feelings for the why. The more your objective gets you juiced, the better your chances are that you'll connect to your audience. Let your humanity (heart) be central to conveying your subject matter (head). Use your head to find your heart or vice-versa. Once these two get together, you'll be compelled to find the objective—the one that gets your passion flowing. Then it's exciting to find the actions that will get you and your audience to the objective. You will take them on a trip with your story, and they will feel compelled to follow.

HEART AND HEAD, OBJECTIVE AND ACTIONS—A CONCRETE EXAMPLE

A good known example of the heading above, is President Obama's Inaugural Address (you can read the Address by Googling it). I would say that his objective was, *to assure* Americans that they will prevail—in their economic crises, their health care problems, their goals around the world, etc. His actions were many: *To evoke* their past, and how they have, "carried on not simply because of the skill or vision of people in high office, but because we, the people, have remained faithful to the ideals of our forebears and true to our founding documents." Other actions could be identified as: *to inspire, to caution, to level, to commiserate*, with the American people, and to recognize some in the audience as examples, to mention a few. All of these actions would be in pursuit of the objective: to assure the American people that they will prevail. It was also delivered with both heart and head.

Sometimes it's not easy getting your heart and head together and revealing yourself. But if you put the work in, the rewards will be more than worth it. As Nelson Mandela once said, "A good head and good heart are always a formidable combination. But when you add to that a literate tongue or pen, then you have something very special."

LOOK ME IN THE EYE AND TELL ME THAT

Many people are afraid of eye contact with the audience, yet it's the most powerful way for their sincerity to reach others. Just think of how you feel when someone doesn't meet your eyes, particularly if it's an important conversation.

If you save practicing eye contact for when you're doing your presentation you will most likely be thrown off in some way—unless you're an experienced speaker who is practiced in it. Many speakers just look around the room and over the heads of the audience as they speak. This is so commonplace that there is an expression for it among professional speakers—it's called, "surfing the room." So if don't want to be a room-surfer, practice this exercise.

EYE CONTACT EXERCISE—USING POST-ITS FOR EYES

The simplest way to approach eye contact is to pick three spots around the room: middle spot, left and right. You can use objects that are in the room, or use Post-its and stick them to various objects. The purpose is to deliver your presentation to the spots, which are, of course, the eyes of your future audience. You can make these spots the audiences' foreheads in the actual speech, but as you get less anxious in your speechmaking, get direct eye contact—looking at their foreheads is much more preferable than surfing the room. You can rearrange where the spots are to suit the layout of your audience if you wish. The important thing is to get your eyes moving to these "people" while you're speaking. If you're not used to it, it can be like tapping your head and rubbing your stomach. Have no fear, I have a remedy that most people have fun with and have told me worked great in the actual presentation. It also works for me.

HANGING OUT

What I'm suggesting is no different than hanging out with your friends and family around a dinner table. You're telling them a story, and you just naturally go from face to face as you're telling the story—you don't want to leave anyone out. If you approach it this way, you won't get hung up on how long you stay with each "set of eyes." You'll just be telling the story and intuitively moving from person to person. Also, you'll move in a non-linear way. That is, you'll skip around rather than go from left to center to right, and vice-versa. You will also be reinforcing the storytelling frame of mind I wrote about earlier. If you're having trouble, or just want to make your eye contact better, you could talk to your spots *as if* each were a specific supportive friend. (Remember, you're not trying to convince yourself that the spot is your friend, just talk to it *as if* it were your friend.) I once worked with a woman who practiced eye contact using her beloved collection of Teddy Bears as her audience. Then she used that feeling of warm familiarity in her actual presentation. Her words (head) conveyed that she meant business, and the Teddy Bears (heart) made the audience listen. It was a great success.

HANDS, AND WHAT TO DO WITH THEM

I rarely teach gestures because they *look* made up and wooden. If you pursue an objective that really moves you, you will move accordingly—and the gestures will be yours. The work I'm proposing in this handbook, as I said in the introduction, is all about bringing out the "you" in you. However, there is one position that I give everyone. It's called the neutral position. Once I describe it to you, you might remember that you've seen lots of spokespeople use it on TV, or you will suddenly start noticing that they use it.

THE NEUTRAL POSITION

Place both hands together in the center of your torso just above your naval. You can use any variation: hands clasped loosely, fingertips touching, etc. The reason why most spokespeople use this position is that it always gives them an unobtrusive home to come back to when they gesture. Many find it a much more active and assertive position than having your hands fall to your sides. Do not play with your ring, or wring your hands. Hands dropped and held together at around your crotch, obviously call attention to that part of your anatomy, and you do not need that—some speakers have this as their neutral position! Once you get used to bringing your hands to the neutral position, I think you will find it very freeing. Your natural gestures flow out from the center of your body and back again, propelling your presentation toward its objective.

HOW TO GIVE SUPER POWERED PRESENTATIONS
When You're Ready to Move to the Next Level

Movement during a speech

If you are in full command of your material and want to move during a speech, the key is to use the movement to make a point and relate more fully to the audience.

For instance, you're transitioning from one section of your speech to another. Let's say you just finished the overview of what your presentation is about, and next you're going to tell the story of how your company got started. As you start to tell the story, you move, at an angle, a few steps left and closer to the audience. This move not only physically marks the transition from the overview to the story of your company, but it brings you closer to the audience. Closer would be a good choice if you wanted to be more personal in this section. You could choose the action, *to confide* your company's story, using a confidential tone by lowering your voice slightly as you move closer. This movement and your unspoken desire *to confide*, will not be lost on the audience, although they probably won't be aware that your movement and the lowering of your voice was what affected them. I have done this countless times and have seen people lean in to hear what I was "confiding."

So movement can help propel your story just as much as gesture can. Unmotivated movement can make your speech less clear and distracting, just as unmotivated gesture can. I'm sure we've all seen the speaker who aimlessly gestures and/or wanders all over the platform, and so our minds begin to wander as well.

PACING AND PAUSING

Many urban people talk too fast. In New York, where I'm based, it's practically a given. Some people talk too slow. And most people give presentations at the same pace and never think of changing pace or pausing—except those who are anxious, and they usually go from too fast to faster. Again, this is a matter of breathing, being relaxed, knowing your objective, and the particular action you have given to the section you are on.

I remember working with a CEO who came to a section of his presentation that described what was phenomenal growth in his company. He recited it at the same pace as the previous section, which was about their meager beginning. I asked him how he felt about the phenomenal growth. He replied he felt excited. I said could he put that excitement in this section and talk slightly faster? Also, would he take a brief pause between each accomplishment his company made, and breathe during these pauses? Finally, I asked him to slow down slightly as he got to the bottom line of all the accomplishments: THE PHENOMENAL GROWTH. He was thrilled at the result. The interesting thing is, even if he weren't excited, what I just described in terms of pacing and pausing would certainly tend to stimulate excitement in the speaker, and if it didn't, would make him *appear* excited.

INFLECTION

If you don't consider yourself a good storyteller, listen and watch someone who is. I can guarantee they're not going to tell the story at one pace, and they're going to pause. Another thing they're going to do is called *inflection*: changes of pitch in their voice to accentuate what they are saying. Many speakers accentuate words by saying them louder, or to put it another way, punching their words. Unfortunately, this tends to make the audience punch-drunk. Inflection captures the audience's ears and makes them want to listen. It's the difference between hearing one note played over and over and hearing a good melody. Listen to a good storyteller (presenter, speaker) and learn to recognize the slight changes in pitch and how they hold your ear. Also, listen to what they choose to inflect. "I *think* it's a good investment," is very different from, "I think it's a *good* investment."

TAKING YOUR SHOW ON THE ROAD

There's an old jazz song that goes:

"There ain't no such thing as the next best thing to love, no reasonable facsimile thereof."

Fortunately, there is a reasonable facsimile for public speaking and we've been doing it. Now comes the actual presentation, and there are a number of practical things to be done so you can have some fun doing what you have been rehearsing.

THE VENUE

Presentations come in all sizes. I've worked with hedge fund and banking people who talk to just a handful of investors in a conference room, as well as fashion companies that are having a bash for an industry audience of five thousand.

No matter what kind of room you're in, find a way to see it beforehand and stand where you would be with a live audience. If you can run some of your presentation, an hour before or the night before, because it's being held in a hotel conference room, convention center, or the like, so much the better—you can try to make arrangements with the staff. If you can't do that because you'll be entering the conference room with everyone else, or they will be there before you, try to cross in front of the audience before you take your seat, and look out at the audience. Why? So that when you come up to address the audience, it won't be the first time you've seen them from the speaker's perspective. Any edge you can get before you speak will help familiarize you.

Eye contact will vary with the size of the room. For most presentations, which are done with small audiences, say, ten to fifty people, you should make direct eye contact with the audience—looking at foreheads is fine for beginners. You are not necessary looking to make contact with every person, but with some persons in every section.

For large rooms or theatre-like spaces where you are a good distance from the audience, you should address all the sections of the audience. This will make each person in each section feel as if you were speaking to him or her. Sound strange? I think many of us have had the experience of standing in a group when someone who was, say, thirty feet away, said something to one of us without mentioning a name. This usually evokes a group response of, "Who me?" You can't tell when you're at a distance which one of you the person is looking at. It's the same with large audiences: Talk to one person in a section and you'll talk to all.

Large audiences bring to mind microphones. Let's see how you can use them to your best advantage.

MICROPHONES

Sometimes the microphone will be fixed in the middle of the lectern. If your audience extends to the extreme left and right, physically adjust yourself when addressing those sections so you're still talking into the microphone. If you just turn your head there will be a falloff in sound—this adjustment usually requires leaning in and pivoting your body, as you turn your head.

With lapel microphones, do not wear them on your lapel. What I just wrote was not a typo. Again, there might be a falloff of volume when you turn to the side opposite the lapel your microphone is on. Wear it in the middle of your upper torso, high on your breastbone, on your blouse or shirt. Women should wear a suit instead of a dress, to accommodate the clipping on of the transmitter to your belt—some are not hi-tech and are heavy.

The following may seem obvious but I assure you, I have seen it happen on many an occasion. If you have a hand-held microphone, do not speak and gesture at the same time with the hand that's holding it. Things like this happen if you're not experienced in holding a microphone. But hand-held microphones can give you wonderful control of volume, and therefore intimacy in a speech. You can hold them close and whisper, or farther away and roar. Watch a seasoned singer on TV work with a hand-held microphone and you'll see what I mean.

LAUGHTER

Some of us are naturally funny.
Some of us can tell a joke.
Most of us can learn *how* to tell a joke.

How to bring on the laughs is something I'll leave to other books—there are many of them. But if you've got them laughing, pause, and start speaking as the laughter subsides. By continuing to speak without pausing, you are, as the comics say, "stepping on your own joke."

MURPHY'S LAW

When I speak in public, I operate under the dictum of Murphy's Law, which states: "If anything can go wrong, it will." So I always troubleshoot a location. Make sure of the sight lines, that is, where you can and cannot be seen. If I am working with a microphone, I will check out the sound beforehand if at all possible. I'll know who to reach if the sound goes. If I'm doing a Power Point presentation I always have a spare projection bulb with me—yes, they have gone on me during a presentation. If you bring your own equipment, call ahead to find out if the venue can accommodate it. In short, look at anything you're working with and ask, what could go wrong with this? Chances are nothing will go wrong, but if it does, you've got a plan.

HAVE FUN

Well, you've done all your work, so go out there and have fun! If you've put your passion into this presentation by finding your objective and pursuing it with juicy actions, you're going to have fun. If you're new to public speaking, it will take a few speeches before you really start to enjoy it. No matter what your given talent, if you follow the teachings in this handbook you will become a good public speaker. This accomplishment will not only bring in business and improve your visibility, but it will make you a better person. Many people have told me this training has improved their communication in relationships outside of work. Some have told me, it changed their lives.

ENCAPSULATION OF EXERCISES

BREATHE YOUR STRESS AWAY
(PGS. 10-11 IN HANDBOOK)

1. Lie down on a mat with your legs supported by pillows, or your knees pointed towards the ceiling and feet flat on the floor.

2. Arms by your sides, close your eyes and relax. Let go of all the tension in your body, starting with the top of your head to your toes. Do this for three minutes, breathing in and out through your nose as you normally would. Timers are helpful and should be very close at hand so you barely have to move.

3. Feel how your stomach is rising and falling with each inhalation and exhalation— familiarize yourself with this feeling.

DIAPHRAGMATIC BREATHING
(PGS. 11-12)

1. Notice that along with your stomach rising and falling your lower ribcage is expanding with the inhalation and contracting with the exhalation.

2. Concentrate on feeling your breath go down into the bottom of your torso and your chest will move less. Gently do this for three minutes. Notice if you feel more relaxed.

OPENING THE "DOORS" (PG. 12)

Exercises to do at anytime, but especially before speaking.

1. Chewing as if you had something especially chewy and delicious in your mouth. Do this for a minute. Sense how your jaw feels before and after.

2. Arms above your head, yawn and stretch your soft palate. Feel the stretch in your soft palate while stretching your whole body. Do this three times. Sense how you feel before and after.

MAKING SOUNDS (PGS. 12-13)

Done lying down, seated, and standing. It's as if the sound were originating from below your naval. The key is to relax and be gentle.

1. HAH-HAH-HAH (breath), HAH-HAH-HAH (breath), HAH-HAH-HAH (breath), etc. Use your hands to check that your breath is going all the way down in your torso. Also, use your hands to check for reverberation (resonance) in your chest and rib cage. You very well might not feel resonance in your lower rib cage at first; just keep thinking the breath down, and don't force it, and you will. Do these exercises for a minute, or more if you're having difficulty, or enjoying your newfound resonance. The feeling that you're looking for in these exercises, is that the sound is coming from your whole torso.

2. Then draw out the sound (chant), holding the A vowel for a few seconds: HAAAAAH (breath), HAAAAAH (breath), HAAAAAH (breath), etc..

3. Lastly, MUM-MUM-MUM (breath), MUM-MUM-MUM (breath) MUM-MUM-MUM (breath) etc.

4. Again draw out the sound, holding the U vowel for a few seconds: MUUUUM (breath), MUUUUM (breath), MUUUUM (breath), etc. Check for resonance because M is such a humming sound. In fact, to get the feeling of strong resonance you can just hum, the lower in pitch the better.

SAYING YOUR FIRST WORDS (PGS. 13-14)

The below is a three-step process: lying down, seated and standing. What you're looking for while seated or standing, is to have your voice sound similar to the way it sounds when you're lying down.

1. Lying down, you speak your opening remarks. Then you chant them, slowly drawing them out. Notice the energy it takes. Then you say them in your normal voice and pace while keeping the energy of the chanting.

2. Seated, as erect as you can without creating tension, do the same as step one.

3. Standing, as erect as you can without creating tension, do the same as step two.

VISUALIZATION (PGS. 19-20)

The purpose of this exercise is to keep you in the present, and not in the future worrying about your presentation.

1. Seated, eyes closed, breathing gently down into your lower torso. Feel yourself: buttocks on the chair, feet flat on the floor, your breathing relaxed and easy.

2. You are imagining yourself in the conference room, or wherever it is you are going to present. You are watching and listening to the person who is introducing you. Remember, you are watching through your eyes, not watching yourself as if you were in a movie. (If you are walking up to the front of the room unannounced then you're doing this exercise a few minutes before you are going to start—in short, you imagine whatever the circumstances will be.)

3. When your mind wanders, just gently bring yourself back to your breathing, feeling yourself in the chair and listening to the speaker.

4. When introduced: *imagine* pushing your chair back, walking to the lectern, be very sure you are breathing, look your greeter in the eye, shake hands and thank them.

5. Imagine turning to face the audience, look at a friendly face somewhere in the middle of the audience, and take a breath. Pick the friendly face before hand. Don't rush the beginning of your presentation: your attitude is *as if* you were welcoming the audience into your home.

DOING WHAT YOU VISUALIZED—WALK TO THE LECTERN (PGS. 20-21)

Next you should physically do what you visualized. In this example, we're going to presume it's a speech given at a lectern. In the room where you are rehearsing set an actual place where the lectern is—you can buy an inexpensive portable music stand to serve as a lectern. Then you should:

1. Imagine that you are being announced (you are breathing, feeling yourself in the chair and watching the spot where you "put" the lectern).

2. Then you actually get up, walk to the lectern, and shake an imaginary hand while looking your "greeter" in the eye.

3. Turn and face the "audience," look at the friendly face you've picked before hand, and take a breath.

4. Start your presentation.

"MAKING MISTAKES" *(PG. 21)*

1. Most mistakes are minor stumbles and are not really noticed.

2. If you make a big deal about it, it *will* be a big deal. But if you take a breath, regain your focus and stay with what you're saying next, instead of your mind being back at the "mistake," you'll be fine. Just keep pursuing your objective.

3. Example of what to say for a totally incomprehensible, really big gaffe: "Wasn't *that* an interesting statement?" There might be laughter—when it starts to subside, "What I meant was…"

You can place a whole speech in front of you for reference. If you do this, I suggest the following.

PREPARING YOUR HARD COPY *(PGS. 23-24)*

1. At least 14 point type so you can refer to it at a glance.

2. In the actual circumstance, do not spend most of your time reading a speech from a script unless you want the audience to only remember the top of your head. So be very familiar with what is on the page.

3. Never staple pages together. Always have two pages in front of you, that way when you're finished with page one you can refer to page two without distracting the audience by noisily turning pages. Also, while you speak from familiarity the words that are on page two, you can soundlessly move it over to the right on top of page one. Again you will have two pages in front of you.

4. In going from one page to another you can break the text in whatever way is most clear to you. I recommend that you mark your text, or highlight it, in places where you have trouble, or want to strongly emphasize.

EYE CONTACT EXERCISE *(PG. 26)*

1. Use post-its and stick them to objects, walls, chairs, or what have you, around the room: middle, left, right.

2. Post-its are used *as if* they are the eyes of the audience. You deliver the presentation to the spots.

3. You can make these spots the audience's foreheads in the actual speech, but as you get less anxious, go for direct eye contact.

4. You can rearrange the spots to suit the layout of your audience, if you know it in advance.

5. As you present, move from spot to spot in no particular order *as if* you were telling a story to friends around a table.

THE VENUE *(PGS. 31-32)*

1. Find a way to see the room beforehand (arrange with hotel staff, etc.) and stand where you will with a live audience. If you can run some or all of your presentation, so much the better.

2. If your audience is in the conference room before you, or you're entering with them, try to cross the speaking area and look out at the audience; that way, when you address the group, it won't be the first time you've seen them from the speaker's perspective.

MICROPHONES *(PG. 32)*

1. If the microphone is fixed to the lectern, don't forget to adjust your body when you turn extreme left or right so there is no falloff in sound—this usually requires leaning in as you turn your head.

2. Lapel microphones are worn high on the breastbone, not on your lapel. Women should wear a suit because of

the clipped-on transmitter for the microphone—some are heavy and not exactly hi-tech.

3. If you have a hand-held microphone, do not gesture and speak at the same time with the hand that's holding it.

LAUGHTER *(PG. 32)*

When you get a laugh, don't forget to pause until the laughter is subsiding, before continuing.

THE PRESENTATION *(RECAP)*

1. Don't forget the jaw exercise (chewing something delicious for a minute). And the stretching exercise (stretching with arms over your head, and yawning to stretch your soft palate). Do this three times. It will also help to relax you. If need be, you can do them in a restroom cubicle, as close to your speaking as possible.

2. *Actually* do what you imagined in your visualization just before going up to speak. When you get in front of the audience, pause and take a breath before you start, looking at a friendly face you've picked out before hand.

3. Have a hard copy, fourteen-point minimum. Or work off your Power Point bullet points or index cards.

4. Remember eye contact—or forehead contact for beginners.

5. Hands in neutral position when not gesturing.

6. You should be familiar with the whole presentation, but have the opening and closing unforgettably memorized.

© *Fred Rivera 2009*

LIST OF VERBS

There are more than two thousand verbs in the English language. Here are a few of them—to help spur you to action.

To:

Charm	Oppose
Challenge	Rouse
Demand	Quash
Reveal	Inform
Plead	Surmount
Implore	Bait
Protest	Excite
Illustrate	Alarm
Cajole	Goad
Grab	Irritate
Command	Provoke
Dominate	Conquer
Titillate	Delay
Tantalize	Compromise
Urge	Placate
Incite	Patronize
Demonstrate	Beguile
Entice	Impress
Pacify	Intrigue
Flatter	Dazzle
Contest	Deflate
Encourage	Inflate
Inspire	Defy
Embrace	Vindicate
Tease	Compare
Confide	Rectify

www.ingramcontent.com/pod-product-compliance
Lightning Source LLC
Chambersburg PA
CBHW041115180526
45172CB00001B/263